Luce Lapadula

The Weekender

LONDON

Volume 2 – Richmond

COLLECTIVE SHORTS
by NHP PUBLISHING

“To my mum, who has always supported my adventures; to my nephew, in the hope that I can inspire him to live a life full of wonders; and to my younger self, who never stopped believing in herself.” – Luce

To me, Richmond is one of the hidden gems that London holds, an oasis within the chaos, where history, grace, and uniqueness converge. It's a place to pause and enjoy the moment. I wanted to create a journey that can guide you through the roads and places that offer a different perspective on London. Richmond is where I find everything I need without stepping into central London. I can shop, enjoy authentic Italian gelato, and spend an entire day in its royal park, exploring the woodland and watching wildlife up close.

Luce Lapadula

Thursday

RICHMOND
OVERGROUND
UNDERGROUND
Richmond
BUS STOP
UNDERGROUND
OVERGROUND
Richmond

Thursday 3 PM Hotel arrival after a taxi ride from Richmond Station

Checking in at the hotel

Thursday 3 PM

Thursday 3:20 PM Admiring the interior design while awaiting the room key

Room details at the Richmond Hotel

Thursday 3:40 PM

Timeless English window Thursday 4:30 PM

VAPE HOUSE
VAPE & CBD
COFFEE
TO LET
OFFICE

THE
RAILWAY
TAVERN
GUINNESS

Thursday 6 PM Dinner at L'Assaggino restaurant in 9 Paved Ct

Friday

BAKERY

Friday 9:30 AM

A sweet breakfast at Richmond Hill Bakery

Strolling through the woods & wonders of Richmond Park Friday 10:30 AM

Landscape of the city center from Sawyer's Hill Friday 11:11 AM

Friday 2:30 PM Walking along the beautiful Richmond Riverside

Making new friends

Chilling by the Tide Table Cafe

The authentic English path of Cholmondeley Walk Friday 3:20 PM

ONE PAVED COURT
ART SPACE & STUDIO
IAT IS LEFT
oline Penn
ther Rigg
28 April

Friday 4 PM Admiring the works by Heather Rigg & Caroline Penn

Friday 7:30 PM

Watching the sunset by Richmond Bridge

DANIELI
TOKO
JEWELLERY

Saturday

Saturday 10:30 AM Strolling through Terrace Gardens before the café

HOLLYHOCK

Enjoying a warm drink at the Hollyhock Café　　Saturday 11 AM

BAILA

The south exit to the gardens Saturday 11:30 AM

SUBWAY TO
TERRACE
GARDENS

Exploring Brewers Lane and Danieli Menswear Saturday 2 PM

Indulging in authentic Italian gelato and chocolates Saturday 2:30 PM

14

Wandering through the Richmond Green area Saturday 3:30 PM

18th-century lodging house, with its charming front porch   Saturday 4 PM

Saturday 6:30 PM Relaxing at the White Swan pub in Old Place Ln

WHITE CROSS

3
6
9

Sunday

Breakfast at the hotel

Sunday 8:30 AM

Sunday 8:50 AM

Decorations in the dining area

Check out

Sunday 10:30 AM

FLOWERS
BRAMB
62
64
FLOWERS
HERBS

& MOSS
FLOWERS

Bramble & Moss flower shop before going to the station Sunday 12 PM

64
FLOWERS
HERBS

The Weekender

LONDON

Volume 2 – Richmond

Published by New Heroes & Pioneers
Photography & text: Luce Lapadula
Creative Direction: Francois Le Bled
Series Book Design: Daniel Zachrisson
Edition Book Design: Lilith Onyett
Model: Charlotte Scrivens

Print and bound by BALTO print (Lithuania)
Legal deposit January 2025
ISBN 9789198656565

MIX
Paper from responsible sources
FSC® C107574
FSC www.fsc.org

"I would like to express my heartfelt thanks to my loved ones, who have encouraged me throughout this journey and reminded me that adventure and photography are at the core of my being. To my friends who have supported and inspired me during this project, your help has been invaluable. A special thanks goes to Charlotte, who rescued me and played a crucial role in bringing this book to life. I am grateful to my editor, François, who believed in my creativity, and to the designers and their team for significantly shaping my vision for this book. I also want to thank those who are part of my daily life for enhancing my perspective on my style, providing comfort, and helping me thrive in my photography career by giving me access to important information. John deserves a special mention for being a guiding light in my life, helping me navigate every version of myself and expand my creativity. Lastly, I extend my thanks to all the contributors who generously supported and trusted me through these pages, and to those who will support my ongoing adventurous journey by exploring this book."

Hotel The Richmond Hill - richmondhill-hotel.co.uk
Restaurant L'assaggino - lassaggino.co.uk
Richmond Hill Bakery
Richmond Park - royalparks.org.uk
Hollyhock Cafe - tidetablescafe.co.uk/hollyhock-cafe/
One Paved Court Gallery - onepavedcourt.co.uk
Danieli Gelaterie - gelateriadanieli.com
Danieli Richmond Clothing
The White Swan Pub - whiteswanrichmond.co.uk
Bramble & Moss Flowers - brambleandmoss.co.uk

COLLECTIVE SHORTS
by NHP PUBLISHING